IRENE LOY

I'VE NAMED THE GODDAMNED RAVENS

COMMON METER PRESS

COMMON METER PRESS
SEATTLE | PORTLAND

COPYRIGHT & PERMISSIONS

Copyright © 2023
Irene Loy, care/of Common Meter Press.

Second paperback edition: November, 2023

Loy, Irene.
I'VE NAMED THE GODDAMNED RAVENS.
First Edition. Seattle: Common Meter Press, 2023. (print)
Subjects: 1. Poetry – spiritual, 2. Creative non-fiction –
memoir, 3. Memoir – pandemic.

ISBN: 979-8-9882494-0-5

To request reprint permissions,
please contact the publisher at
contact@commonmeterpress.com

Printed and Bound in Seattle, WA
at Common Meter Press
2009 NW 62nd St
Seattle, WA 98107

.   .   .

GET MORE POETRY AT

COMMONMETERPRESS.COM

"There's a science to walking through windows without you
all of my thoughts of you
bullets through rotten fruit
come apart at the seams
now I know what dying means"

- GRACELESS, THE NATIONAL

.   .   .

"I think now that maybe true sweetness
can only happen in limbo."

- PETER HELLER

INVOCATION OF POWER

With my Inner Beloved
I go down to the river.

Here I am, marrying Air.

I ask him a question.
He speaks to me, humbles me, praises me.
Mostly he says, "It's not time for you to know yet."

He offers me goat cheese, red wine, honey.
I receive.

He says, "Look how unbothered the river is."
I say, "Yes, but what is the answer?"
He tells me a joke.
I laugh, and tears of joy come out the sides of my eyes.

We make love,
          and I forget my question.

Then, as I rest with him by the river,
                              distracted,
He drops the answer
          silently between my lips.

MY DIVORCES

My divorces
        like a double death
        before I die

But they're mine -

Rolling them about on my tongue like ash
They're a sooty meal,
        and nothing I ordered

My longing for a love affair with myself
        turns my blue moon to gold

But I'm still drinking and smoking too much
        in this sacred-profane
        space of grace,
        my head leaning on the john door
        because I might throw up.

CLOSE YOUR EYES

Close your eyes
and when the time is ripe
Love will reveal to you
the secrets of your heart.

Love - patient, kind - can wait.

Rest, Love, and for now:
            eat this peach.

DISCOMFORT/GLORY

Sun rising slowly
We're drunk, me and my Beloved
      run down to the water
      the brush cutting our naked calves
The water spraying our faces
      as we descend the staircase
I might die from joy
      my love my love my Love
Touch my hair
      and kiss my tears away
We fall, swim in the tumult
      climb out again
It's perilous and worth every breath
I'm gaining in unease, discomfort
      and transition ever present
      in glory, glory, Glory!

TAOS, MY DESCENT PLACE

Taos, my descent place

Ravens cawing
      outside my window
      announcing more death
      I'll have to leave this place I love
      and which repulses me

Mourning the past
      dreaming up the future
      I love this air
      I don't want to leave these trees

I'VE NAMED THE GODDAMNNED RAVENS

This summer, I started planning for my death
      with DeVargas Funeral Home
      like a good, strong INFJ
      who shops local

I moved to Taos and lost a spouse
      my Granny, and two lovers
      I'd like my ashes spread here
      I've died here already, before death

I've died a spiritual death here
      upon my ascent I must admit I'm leaving
      like hiking the Slide Trail
      to memorize the feeling of YES:
      I can climb back out of this gorge in my life.

I want to summer here endlessly
    in this portal, this liminal space of self-quarantine
    Perhaps autumn chill will kick me out -

Life will never be the same on the other side.

ONE MORE HERM

I ascend
        this roadside, rockscape wonderland
        picking up pieces of the mountain
        and placing them on itself

Herm after herm
        leading to some unseen summit
        tired and parched, I turn
        admit, it's time to return to my car

As I prepare to descend
        I feel them behind me
        perhaps one more herm
        one more herm

As if I could ever fully know this place
        but New Mexico is a fathomless ocean
        it will never be revealed to anyone
        in its totality

And my love for it
        will not keep it from lovingly pushing me out

Last week
        on a bench in a courtyard
        I had a sudden urge
        to stuff my shirt with dirt

To make love to this place
        to eat it whole
        keep it in my cells
        I love you, Taos

And you repulse me
        you will forever be a love
        and a past lover of mine

So I will exit
to create
   - Universe willing -

A new chapter of my life

SEA/SALT/TEARS

Oh, this.
    I've done this.
        turning back to behold my past
    like Ado did
the salt she became was undoubtedly tears

    Or sea water
    Those little pillars

Why do we treat the metaphors
    even the obvious ones
        in the Bible
    like such mysteries?
I explain this as to children because I'm crying now

Sorry, I've been a wreck lately
    falling to pieces even
        while following the will of god
    doubts: the chocolate chips in the cookies of faith
Now there's a metaphor we can all follow

I've come apart
    excuse me
        I'll just - (grabbing a piece of herself from the
ground in front of you)
    my past gone - my future as yet unformed
Limbo has a way of wrecking a woman

Please be patient
        even while I'm not
                fears came up this week, jitters, anxiety cubed
        just before the outgoing tide comes back in and -
A wave crystallizes me where I stand.

A LEAVING

She braided her hair the morning she left me
       washed it in that cocoa butter shampoo I love
       braided it still wet
       held up its bottom to complain of split ends
       sat on the edge of my bed
       poised to stand
       hesitating?
       and then walked out without a word
       half-waving to me from the doorway
       as if it were nothing.

ON GHOSTING

I fight it
It is not communication,
     so I feel no need to learn its rules
     yet its rules are imposed on me:

        1. One can ghost another they've been very close to.
        2. When one declares a ghosting game, the other is beholden
        to it./must comply.
        3. An ashy cliff ensues.
        4. I, a Fool, step off it.

WHICHEVER PATH
(A CALIFORNIA POEM)

The heart that follows this path
      is broken
I nurse it
      get up - read maps - go to bed
      go for daily walks
      pause on the path to discover crocuses
          another yellow!
Try to find the place to plant myself
      when what I have is a(nother) gathering urge to leave
I just need one corner to make this hearthfire in
      where it feels true
Yet uprootedness feels more true at the moment
My presence here is my own response
      to all this heartache

I hear
    'You could go to any spot and it would be fine'
    yet I'm 20 spots in now
    a leopard roaming
We are what we are searching for

What map am I following?
    going off the map
Hindsight shows me where I've been
    accumulating fortunes I don't (yet)
    realize by doing this work

Well, labor is work.
Giving birth is work.

HOW TO SPEAK THE COUNTRY INSIDE ME

The official languages of the country inside me
  are Enthusiasm
  and Sadness at unmet ideals.

German and English, too,
  but like the grantig quality of Austrian German
  or the "spend time" commercialism of English,
  the tone of my country's languages is critique.

An urge to live abroad,
  somewhere better than this
  but it isn't time yet

So I move my country-body
  around this Americanah
  and I am often not amused,
  but disheartened

All the ideals we brought here -
  how did we so profoundly miss the mark?

All this pavement, so many strip malls -
  we forgot that people matter more than money

So the citizens of my inner country are crying,
  wondering where to locate this country
  inside of that one.

PEACE

Peace
      - that slope
           into my own anger

      I hated his never-ending silence!

   I threw large stones into his calm lake!

Lack of conversation
         is drought
            is no love

      I became the keeper of the peace
          the one who controlled my speech
             and hands

I chastise myself
     you're covered in thick cloud
         forever pining after a love that is not there

When this - this pen
        this thought
        this cup of tea
        rises up to meet you

Like all the solutions to the problems of absence in your new home
You project all these images of love
     when everything great in the man you love
              you have manufactured

MUST THE MYSTIC SHED AGAIN?

Descend
     descend
          descend

Inanna
     down to the bottom of Hell
          shedding something intensely valuable at each gate

Until She
     naked
          sobbing
               alone

    is all Woman grieving and bone.

Hanging on a hook on the wall

     the Hanged Woman
          nurses the baby,
               her own future

    until her friend helps her claw her way back from death.

Like Cixous
     women giving birth to ourselves
          over and over again

A TILTING WITHIN MYSELF
(A SANTA FE POEM)

This pine tree growing thick in my trunk
>has sprouted one tiny little root here

It doesn't mind commitments

It stands still, unwavering
>and waits for me to tilt toward it
>to quiet the mind
>move back and down
>where the sweetest shoot is growing
>down toward the soil from my tailbone.

I - inexplicably, and with reverence - relent.

PSYCHOPOMP LOVE

Six of Swords
        Psychopomp
            Trickster-Ferryman
                rowing his little boat across the River Styx

The first time we cross, descending, I'm worried, shrouded
        the second time
           my head is held high
              I've learned something, been coached by
midnight and darkness

The ascent has made my tear ducts puffy
        grieving all this loss
           I open doors and find no one
                no one
                no one

While the Buddhist monks sweep the sand painting away
        I twirl my fingers in the water
           wonder at the woman now reflected there

I love this psychopomp
        without whom I would've merely sat on the shoreline
           and died

I am filled with love for this crossing,
and crossing back now
        toward a dawning

I am on the verge of my own personal resurrection

TRICKSTER AT OUR EVENT

Is it wrong that
        I chuckle when
                after all our careful planning
                the wind blows all our
                table seatings away?

LOVING PETER PAN

1.
My mind said,
Do not love this man
      who is incapable of loving you back
But the love came anyway
      and set up a little nest in my heart
I fed it peaches
      and bread
      until it grew so big
It flowed out of my eyes
      when I looked at you
      marvelous fireworks display
All I saw was the beauty
      the handsome
I hoped for you to be a man
      as you told me, you're a Peter Pan
      and your goofy red tennis shoes
      belied your teenage approach to feeling
A running, running
      toward your damn freedom
      and away from the love that came out of me
      as you were slipping beyond the hope of touch.

2.
Forgive me, but I'm not sure how I'm supposed to love anybody else
      after an experience like that
Of falling through the clouds
      like FKA Twigs after piercing the dragon's face with her
stiletto

Tattooed Beauty,
    you loom large in my consciousness now
        when you may be unable to love me back.

3.
All my life for those two hours Wednesday night
All the bridges I've burned lighting the way –
I'm a carnie at heart and should be running a festival

Arms up around this glorious man's neck like aspiration
        just enough light to watch him enter me
        I turn my head aside in glory –

Foolish woman, loving those who can't love you back
        crying inside my mask
        in a courtyard built atop Native graves.

4.
I love you
        like I love fireworks
        from a distance
        jaw-dropped
        in awe of you
        always shooting into space
        colorful, vibrant

You, like fireworks, are unable to love me back.

It's alright
I get shy anyway, teary,
        unsure what to say
        to such a series of bright lights

who, at night,
makes even the sun look small.
I am in love with my romantic notions of you
shocked to be out in public
acknowledging this much beauty.

5.

You hand me stickers
like a child
of the 80's
your flyers
and magnets
until I feel small

6.

This is my full surrender
to your speed
Me, snagging windows of time

Trying to catch your eye
while you look past me

You beautiful tattooed Sag

I buy new bathing suits and bras
that you don't notice

Sit dumbstruck
while you don't ask me questions

You feel affection for me now
I can tell

There's this shared gratitude
      that we can still be together
      and then
      you're off again

Giving me nothing

I develop a thesis
      you know nothing about

Work some job
      it's hardly relevant
      when you're off again

Quick drink before you go -

And if I love you still

      then that's my own damn fault.

I SHOW MY AUNT

I show my Aunt
        this place that pains me
        that breaks my heart

A series of beautiful sights
        and inconveniences,
New Mexico
        has already disenchanted me
        before she had a chance to make it out.

I hit my head
                    God dammit!
Will this place ever work for me?
        I've returned to answer this question.

I try to be a good host
        while encountering a thousand memories
        of loss.

These are a few of my favorite things
        even though

        I still hate my job
        don't know what to do about my rent
        I'm contemplating adding another nine months
        to this long goodbye.

Something feels like it's concluding
        letting me go
        again.

I long for my calling, like a lover
  and sit here alone
  smoking cigarettes on my patio
  (once a week)

The pandemic times,
  a transformational leaving
  and staying
  I'm given no answers yet.

And the clock is ticking on my lease

I hate my job
  did I mention that?
It is so wrong for me.
BUT I could reframe it!
Some series of boring tasks I do eight hours a day
  before soaring
  into my studies

A new crush
  someone I could love

I hope I haven't ruined my chances of being loved.

I've been poisoned here
  you know?
I've taken in the energy of
  a Madman
  an Alcoholic
  and a Peter Pan

A man who,
      when asked if he loved me,
      batted the word away
      like a fly

He said,
      You can just lose track of me altogether

My losses have scabbed over
      I don't pick at them anymore
      because I'm sick of bleeding

The ravens know me now,
      and I've made their acquaintance!

Trying to prove to her, I've learned something -

I show my Aunt
      this place that pains me
      that breaks my heart

A series of beautiful sights
      and inconveniences,
New Mexico
      has already disenchanted me
      by the time she had a chance to make it out.

. . .

ABOUT IRENE LOY

Irene Loy is a PhD Candidate in Creative Research with Transart Institute/Liverpool John Moores University. She holds an MFA in Dramatic Writing from the University of New Mexico and an MA in Speech and Hearing Sciences from Indiana University-Bloomington.

She has written several plays, countless poems, and plenty of creative nonfiction. She has published online with *Sol Forte: A Journal for Spiritual Writing*, *HowlRound*, *Elephant Journal*, *Truity*, and *Live Taos*.

Irene has served as the Research and Communications Director for Improv Medicine, an applied improv LLC based in Taos, since 2016.

She hails originally from Indianapolis (born and raised) and has lived in Canberra, Vienna, New York City, and Boston, as well as in a handful of cities and towns across New Mexico since 2009.

She is on the verge of her own personal resurrection. In the meantime, she enjoys high desert hiking, improvising, and eating blackberry pie.

You can find more about Irene online at ireneloy.com or follow her on Instagram at @ireneathome.

ACKNOWLEDGEMENTS

Thank you to Meredith Smith, my Publisher at Common Meter, for believing in this project and seeing it through with me. And thanks to my good friend Andy Jones* for connecting us.

Thank you to my fellow Kenyon alum, Benjamin Bagocius, for his phenomenal writing group meetings over Zoom through months of the pandemic, during which several of these poems were developed, and for his online *Sol Forte* journal, where many of these pieces were first published.

Thank you, too, in very concrete ways, to my ex-husbands, Jürgen Jung and Scott Edward Lestage - and all of the people I've lost along the way - who helped me to see how very much I needed to be alone to finally grow up in this strange world.

COLOPHON

Our masthead includes:
Editorial Director, Meredith Smith

A micropress based in Seattle and Portland, Common Meter strives to create spaces for multidisciplinary work centered around poetry and music. Offering traditional chapbooks, songbooks, and writers who often play in other forms, Common Meter is a unique voice among indie presses.

.   .   .

CREDITS

This book was digitally printed on FSC-certified paper, with cover-stock in 110 lb Mohawk fine papers. Each book is printed, collated, and pressed by hand in the Common Meter Press studio in the Heart of Ballard.

The very first edition of I'VE NAMED THE GODDAMNED RAVENS was published in July of 2023.

The galley was set in Georgia and Avenir. The Common Meter Press masthead was set in Avenir Bold and American Typewriter. This book, including cover and interior matter, was designed by Meredith Smith.

We recognize that we work on unceded land of the Coast Salish, Duwamish, and indigenous Northwest peoples.

OUR POETRY TITLES

The Fleeting Art of Letting Go
GOSIA ROKICKA – 2024

Beauty Exasperated:
Poems After George Eliot
CASS GARISON – 2024

Grating, Darling, Full of Dirt:
Poems After Stephen King
ERIN DORNEY

Quad Poems: 4-Page Poems
D.E. MORGAN

I've Named the
Goddamned Ravens
IRENE LOY

what are we fighting for?
RILEY SPICER

Maybe I'm Ready to Talk
About What Happened
MEREDTH SMITH

COMMON METER PRESS
SEATTLE | PORTLAND

Printed in the USA
CPSIA information can be obtained
at www.ICGtesting.com
JSHW040749190524
63149JS00001B/4